YOUR KNOWLEDGE HAS VALUE

- We will publish your bachelor's and master's thesis, essays and papers

- Your own eBook and book - sold worldwide in all relevant shops

- Earn money with each sale

Upload your text at www.GRIN.com
and publish for free

Komiete Tetteh

The Pros and Cons of Privatization

A Critical Assessment

GRIN Verlag

Bibliografische Information der Deutschen Nationalbibliothek:

Die Deutsche Bibliothek verzeichnet diese Publikation in der Deutschen National-
bibliografie; detaillierte bibliografische Daten sind im Internet über http://dnb.d-
nb.de/ abrufbar.

Imprint:

Copyright © 2013 GRIN Verlag GmbH
Druck und Bindung: Books on Demand GmbH, Norderstedt Germany
ISBN: 978-3-656-53745-8

GRIN - Your knowledge has value

Der GRIN Verlag publiziert seit 1998 wissenschaftliche Arbeiten von Studenten, Hochschullehrern und anderen Akademikern als eBook und gedrucktes Buch. Die Verlagswebsite www.grin.com ist die ideale Plattform zur Veröffentlichung von Hausarbeiten, Abschlussarbeiten, wissenschaftlichen Aufsätzen, Dissertationen und Fachbüchern.

Visit us on the internet:

http://www.grin.com/

http://www.facebook.com/grincom

http://www.twitter.com/grin_com

The Pros and Cons of Privatization: A Critical Assessment

By
Komiete Tetteh

Abstract

This paper critically discuses the benefits and costs of privatization as well as its success factors and future prospects. Following a snap conceptual review of privatization, including its various forms and reasoning underlying its promulgation as the most effective mechanism for organizing the delivery of public services, it examines in-depth the arguments for and against privatization, and ascertain these claims from actual examples of implemented privatization programs. Evaluating the determinants of successful (and unsuccessful) privatization, it demonstrates the importance of context in shaping the decision, form and likely outcomes of any privatization policy. It is argued that privatization has and will remain an important item on the reform agenda of many governments as a pragmatic solution to deepening domestic challenges, including depleting state revenues and bloating public expenditure, as well as external opportunities and constraints such as foreign direct investments and pressures from international organizations, rather than pure ideological reasons. At the same time, however, given the limitations of privatization, it is asserted that more mixed ownership arrangements or Public-Private-Partnerships (PPP) will assume the face of future privatization.

Key words: privatization, policy, public-private partnerships, liberalization, efficiency.

1. Introduction: The Growth of Modern Privatization

Few would disagree with the notion that privatization has become the most popular ingredient of, or catchphrase for, public sector reforms in the world today. The modern wave of privatization, which gathered momentum in the last quarter century with the rise of right-wing governments in Europe and America[1], coinciding with the end of the cold war following a period of expansive, post-World War II nationalistic, growth and welfare-minded states, had, by the turn of the 21st

---

[1] Perhaps the only exceptions are the few remaining totalitarian states such as North Korea and Sudan, where any hint of change is viewed with skepticism and rejected by their ruling despot as a 'Western conspiracy' calculated to destabilize their society and culture.

century, virtually permeated all corners of the globe—featuring in myriad economic and public sector reform programs in different countries and economies[2]: developed, developing; capitalist, socialist, communist; democratic, authoritarian, etc. Beginning with the sale of state-owned enterprises to private entities or through share issue, the scale and scope of contemporary privatization has expanded dramatically over the years, engulfing almost every aspect of the bureaucratic sector, including the provision of such traditional 'public' services as law enforcement and the most residual of state activities (e.g., revenue collection), with significant social, economic and political ramifications.

Although privatization has been a feature of bureaucratic organization since time immemorial[3], the nature, scale, scope and speed of modern-day privatization is, however, without precedent, thus making it one of the most deliberated, yet contentious public policy and management issues today. While privatization's proponents often cite numerous efficiency gains and better performance outcomes resulting from the denationalization of previously moribund public enterprises or services, opponents however point to several instances of failed privatization initiatives, where promised benefits were not (fully) realized or the social cost of privatization became high. Yet notwithstanding the persistent hostility toward any new privatization policy everywhere, and despite numerous cases of less or unsuccessful privatization, privatization still appears to be the most popular and viable policy option available to many governments today facing multiple challenges. So what factors account for the resurgence of interest in privatization particularly today? And, given recent conservatorship trends in pro-market states such as the USA following the late 2000s financial crisis and the revival of nationalism in places such as South America, is privatization likely to increase or decrease in the near future?

---

[2] Often referred to as 'Thatcherism' and 'Reaganomics', respectively describing the economic policies of former UK prime minister Margaret Thatcher (1979-90), whose recent passing away rekindled the debate about her legacies; and that of Ronald Regan, US president, 1981-89. Thatcherism and Reaganomics are characterized by privatization, deregulation, tax breaks, small government, constraints on labour movement, and tight control of monetary supply, also known as supply-side economics, in contrast to Keynesianism (i.e., demand-stimulus economics) which was the main policy instrument used by governments. But perhaps rather than simply interpret their actions purely from an ideological lens, it may be useful to consider the conditions that led to the implementation of those policies: high unemployment, stagflation and high government deficits.

[3] The history of civilizations is littered with several examples of private sector participation in the function of the command or bureaucratic unit of society. Ancient Greek, the Roman Republic and China under Han dynasty all had private individuals and companies perform essential functions, such as tax collection, construction, etc for or on behalf of the state. Moreover, even prior to the modern wave of privatization, governments (both local and national) in different countries had certain responsibilities delegated to the private sector. Examples include water distribution in France and provision of emergency services in Denmark by private companies.

1

I interrogate these issues in this paper, which aims to critically examine the merits and demerits of privatization, with particular attention to 'full' privatization, ascertain the reasons underlying its proliferation, and offer an assessment of its future prospects. Following a snap conceptual review of privatization, including its many approaches and the reasoning underlying its promulgation as the most effective mechanism for organizing the delivery of public services (section 2), I examine in-depth the arguments for and against privatization, and verify these claims from actual examples of implemented privatization (section 3). Next, I demonstrate the importance of context in shaping the decision, form and likely outcomes of any privatization policy (section 4), and argue pragmatically that privatization has and will remain an important item on the reform agenda of many governments (section 5), concluding, though, that more mixed ownership arrangements or Public-Private-Partnerships (PPP) will assume the face of future privatization.

2. Privatisation: A Brief Conceptual Overview

2.1 Meaning

The term privatization is often used to mean different things[4]. However, in conventional political and economic sense, privatization either connotes a shift, total or partial, in any activities or functions previously performed by the state to non-state actors[5]. In other words, it is the limited or absolute ceding of the government responsibilities for production and provision to the private sector. Privatization is intrinsically linked to, but distinct from, deregulation, commercialization, and corporatization, which entails the exposure of the public sector to market principles.

Deregulation, which is also known as liberalization, is the relaxation or removal of government rules and regulations to allow enable private companies operate in area/sector previously open to the public sector alone. Commercialization is where a public company is given full autonomy to operate like a private one (in respect of operations, management and application of business-type decisions), without many changing ownership. Under corporatization, the public enterprise is

---

[4] Privatization can refer to any of the following: a term or idea of withdrawing from the 'whole' or 'collective' to 'part' or 'specific', such as a shift in expenditure from public health (e.g., vaccination) to private medical care (Starr, 1989); an anti-interventionist movement generally opposed to government regulation; right-wing political thought or conservatism; or an actual policy instrument that alters the relational dynamics between the command or bureaucratic module and the non-bureaucratic unit of society, often by increasing the latter's role in the organization of the state, as upheld above. But as will become clearer in the next section, even within the policy framework, privatization can be used to pursue a range of goals that are different. Besides, it is becoming increasingly evident that the boundaries between what was traditionally considered 'private' and 'public' is becoming blurred.

[5] These include both for-profit and non-profit entities.

given the legal status of a private company, although government still retains ownership. These three (successive) approaches may serve as a precursor to full privatization, which is when ownership becomes private.

2.2 Forms

Privatization can take several, if not inexhaustible, forms, such that it is better viewed as a continuum, ranging from very limited privatization (e.g., petty trading in Cuba), to large-scale privatization whereby ownership and management of major corporations or a sector of the economy is dominated by the private sector, such as the airline industry in the USA. That said, however, we can classify all the different forms of privatization into two major typologies, based on governments' in or non-involvement in the ownership, management and financing of the resulting organization or delivery mechanism: full and partial privatization.

Full privatization - this is where governments, which can be national, regional or local, divests themselves of public enterprises or services and transfers their ownership and responsibility (including related risks) into private hands through trade sale, share flotation, voucher issue or liquidation.

Partial privatization - for partial or incomplete privatization, the state bequeaths some of its functions or assets to the private sector while retaining some amount of control, ownership or oversight. Examples of incomplete privatization are:

1. *Contracting out* - this is where certain services (e.g., garbage/revenue collection) are given to private companies who bid for them in return for payment;
2. *Joint Venture* – this is where part of government assets or equity in public enterprise is sold to the private sector, resulting in joint ownership;
3. *Subsidizing people* through the use of vouchers (e.g., food/tuition stamps) to purchase a good or service at market price from private suppliers;
4. *Subsidizing companies* to supply goods and services directly to consumers.

Other forms of partial privatization include: *management privatization,* where management responsibility is handed to the private sector while retaining public ownership; *franchising,* which entails granting monopoly rights to a private company or a number of them to supply a good or service; and *leasing*, whereby public assets (e.g., land, infrastructure, etc) is rented to a private company to provide a good or service for a specific time period.

2.3 Theoretical Underpinnings

Several theories have been used to justify and explain privatization. While libertarianism and its variants, including neoliberalism and lazier faire economics[6], could be seen as the meta theory or ideology supplying privatization's moral philosophy, concepts such as principal-agent problem, property rights approach, and public choice economics offer diagnostic and explanatory analysis pertaining to the inherent shortcomings of bureaucratic organization from a structural perspective. Principal-agent theory, for example, attributes the public sector's underperformance to the disconnect between the interests of citizens or taxpayers (i.e. the principal) and that of politicians, bureaucrats and public enterprise managers (i.e., the agent who have been hired to manage public resources on their behalf), and the former's inability or difficulty in ensuring that their interests are catered to by the latter, due to problems of information asymmetry, contract incompleteness as well as high transaction costs and risks entailed. Similarly, public choice theory[7], which sees all public officials, like individuals and voters, as rational, self-seeking, utility-maximizers, and points to the effects of the reward system in public service (e.g., tying performance to output, budget size, staff strength) as well as political conditions and constraints (rent-seeking, clientelism, coalitions, elections, etc) in encouraging officials' mismanagement of public resources, to satisfy selfish political or personal ambitions at the expense of the greater social good (e.g. cost control or reduction, equity, productivity improvement), and advocate ways of aligning 'public' interests with the incentives of public workers, which privatization provides—a position also adopted by the property rights school, which, highlighting the difficulty in capturing returns on asserts, excluding and transferring property rights under public ownership, espouses privatization as the only way of reassigning property rights to incentivize efficiency, cost reduction and innovation.

---

[6] Although these ideas differ in their fine details about the vision of what the ideal society should be, the common thread that weaves through all them is their belief in: free choice, limited government, the superiority of the public sector over the private sector in terms of production and management, and rationale, self-maximizing individual behaviour of all people.

[7] In part, public choice theory emerged as a critique of the Webarian ideal bureaucratic model, which assumes that 'official' resources, conduct and interests can be insulted from 'private' or personal incentives, and as lacking cost consciousness due to the weak connection between cost and output, which it gives excessive attention to (Labi, 2003)

The third set of theories which are tied to privatization include transaction-cost theory, New Public Management, contract and procurement theory, which provide the guidelines, tools and techniques for implementing privatization. However, unlike the other theories above, these theories do not advocate privatization as the panacea to the problems of the public sector, but a contingency based approach that may include the market or bureaucracy or elements of both. For example, transaction-cost theory, associated with Williamson (1985), for instance, asserts that contracting out is more efficient in conditions where goods supply can be contested, specifications (quantity and quality) can be made and measured, and supply is competitive; on the other hand, in-house provision is preferable where transactions are characterized by uncertainty, complexity and special skills, and where quality is crucial and the threat of opportunism exit (Bale and Dale, 1998). Similarly, New Public Management postulates that the challenges and performance of both public and private organization can be solved or improved by the application of a distinct activity: management. Thus, it prescribes a repertoire of 'business' principles for improving organizational performance, including a departure from input control, rules and adherence to procedures toward output measurement and performance targets, and replacing traditional 'tall' hierarchies with flatter, more flexible structures designed around specific processes rather than traditional functions (Bale and Dale, 1998; Labi, 2003)

3. The Case for and Against Privatization

The wider arguments used to support and oppose privatization can be stated as follows. Economically, adherents claim that privatization, at the micro level, increases efficiency and productivity, enhances product or service quality, expands the range of choice to consumers, spurs innovation, cuts cost, reduces prices, and raises firm profits through the combination of the right incentives, curtailed political interference, competition, reinvestment, greater accountability and control mechanisms to ensure value for money. At the macro-level, it generates direct cash from asset sale[8]; develops or increases the capitalization of local stock markets as new companies list; and, above all, improves government fiscal health, boots employment and contributes to economic growth by eliminating 'wasteful' spending, reducing borrowing requirements and 'crowding-out', attracting foreign investments, and generating new revenues from new corporate or income taxes. Critiques, however, argue that privatization often creates

---

[8] For example, proceeds from the government of Ghana's state enterprises divestiture program amounted to 14% of GDP between 1987-1993 (see Appiah-Kubi, 2001).

local monopolies, especially in utilities, who often exploit their market power to harm consumer welfare by reducing output and raising prices or profits, as happened in Guinea's water sector (Nellis, 2005). They also point to other market failures associated with privatization such as public goods, negative externalities, imperfect information, and claim that, in many (developing) nations, divested assets are acquired by foreigners, who funnel bulk of their profits outside the country without making any significant local investments, socially and economically—thus, adding no real benefits to the economy.

Socially, privatization eliminates or reduces public sector corruption, removes unnecessary red-tape, increases institutional sensitivity to consumer tastes and improves customer service, supporters say. Ownership of (shares in) privatized state companies empowers citizens and increases their overall participation in the management of the economy, as evidenced by the over 200% jump in shareholding Brits under Thatcher's privatization policy, while social spending, it is added, can be (re)prioritized, sometimes to mitigate the negative effects of privatization. But opponents insist that privatization exacerbates rather reduces social inequality, often by: turning the 'social service' imperative of public services, such as utilities, into profit-making incentives, thereby denying access to, or worsening the plight of, the poor, as seen in the aftermath of Bolivia's 1990s water privatization—a human rights issue; concentrating wealth in the hands of a few (e.g, Russia's post-privatization oil oligarchs); and inflating unemployment due to the massive retrenchment that usually follows liquidation and privatization of state companies, as was witnessed in Ghana.

The moral and political arguments favouring privatization include increase in personal freedom resulting from the reduction in state activities, as seen in China today, and administrative/fiscal decentralization, also visible in former communist states and military dictatorships, including Poland and Chile, seen as the precursor to democracy. But here again, detractors cite political opportunism, use of privatization to further clientele politics and regulatory capture by new companies—in effect, transforming but not eliminating corruption, as seen in many African countries. They also mention institutional fragmentation, which hampers coordination, creates confusion and gaps in service delivery, thereby affecting overall service efficiency, as was the case after Britain's rail privatization, while others interpret the sale of strategic national assets (e.g., airports), especially to foreigners as morally indefensible and loss of national sovereignty.

6

Closing this section, it is important to underscore the following points. First, privatization, as can be inferred from above, is often used as a means to different ends and triggers multiple impacts, often beyond the formal scope of its stated objectives. Second, some of privatization's theoretical justifications are debatable—for example, public choice theory's conjecture that self-motive underlines all collective action has been refuted by sociologists and institutional economists such as Lars Udehn and Ha-Joon Chang, who cite other non-selfish incentives behind public policy (see Udehn, 1996; Chang, 2000). Similarly, Ouchi (1980) has demonstrated the efficacy of the 'clan' mode of control in resolving the principal-agent problem in bureaucracy, accounting for the high efficiency of state-owned enterprises in places such as Japan, while other studies have proven that the property right thesis about the superiority of private ownership is weak under sufficient competition. Third, while some of the outputs and impacts of privatization (e.g. shares sold, deficit reduction) may be quantifiable, tangible and immediate, others (e.g. personal liberty, welfare gains) may be less measurable and long-term, implying that the time of evaluation is crucial. Fourth, in reality, both proponents and opponents can find a litany of successful and failed privatization programs to buttress their respective positions on the matter, with varying degrees of weight. Fourth, no privatization policy will yield the same consequences everywhere. Therefore, any attempt at judging the effectiveness of a particular privatization policy must not only consider these factors, but also include an appreciation of the context in which privatization occurred, which leads me to the next section.

4. Evaluating Privatization's Success: The Important of Context

The way in which the policy of privatization is conceived, designed and implemented, and the political, economic, social and institutional milieu in which it occurs (Howlet and Ramesh, 1995; Flynn 2002) can have profound effect on its expected benefits: firm/service efficiency, distributional impact, and economic performance. For example, during financial crisis, privatization can become the prism for resolving or escaping short-term economic crisis, without giving adequate attention to, and planning for, its long-term implications. That is to say, many governments resort to privatization as a means of raising cash from the sale of assets and or satisfying lender or donor conditions for receiving aid, loan or debt cancellation. However, in most cases, the problem of debt continue to persist, if not becoming worse, as governments have to cope with the failed expectation of wooing huge investments from abroad and revenues from liquidized asserts. By extension, self-engineered privatization, such as New Zealand's, is more

7

likely to receive local support or face less opposition than externally-imposed privatization, as is happening Greece today.

These two sources of the privatization policy resonate with DiMaggio and Powel's description of the causes of organizational change; namely, 'coercive isomorphism', where the source of change emanates from powerful outside forces (e.g., the IMF, World Bank) exerting pressure on the receiving entity to conform to their view of what the ideal type or structure ought to be, and 'mimetic isomorphism', which is a self-initiated reform undertaken to adopt the form of another organization perceived as the best, in the face of uncertainty. This point speaks well to the fundamental reason for the failure of many externally-crafted and imposed policies, including privatization, in developing countries which are transferred from other jurisdictions without recourse to the cultural, social and political context of the receiving nations, and serves as source of frustration to initiators (see Schick, 1998).

Also, in situations where there are few suppliers and buyers for the goods or service to be privatized, as is the case in most African countries, the likelihood of opportunism (Ouchi, 1980) and monopoly formation is high than, say in New Zealand, where the market was already vibrant prior to privatization (Schick, 1998)[9]. As well, asset-disposal methods that promote 'popular capitalism' (e.g., voucher) will gain broader local support than those that produce 'crony capitalism' or oligarchy (e.g., sale to foreign or domestic political elites).

Similarly, the quality of the institutional environment before (including definition/protection of property rights), during (e.g., investment laws, process transparency) and post-privatization (i.e., regulatory framework) will influence local perceptions, investor confidence, level of service, and user satisfaction with the outcome of privatization. In addition, if adequate measures are put in place to deal with the environmental and social cost of privatization, the degree of local acceptance will be higher than if no such policies existed. Lastly, the way in which privatization

---

[9] Guriev and Megginson (2005) compare the connection between privatization and strong institutions in countries with weak institutions to the 'chicken and egg' scenario. They argue that, on one hand, countries with weak institutions are the ones that demonstrate a greater need for privatization because of poor institutional performance; yet these are the ones least able to implement successful privatization polices due to the 'poverty' of their institutions. This is similar to the connection between privatization and markets. It is said that privatization thrives in places where the market sector is already developed, compared to missing or undeveloped markets (see Williamson; Ochi, 1980; Gauld, 2003). Yet the market cannot be developed without privatization. These constitute the major explanation for the poor performance of privatization policies in developing nations, compared to their developed counterparts.

is packaged and rolled out will hugely impact on its success. If it is implemented in a piecemeal, sequential fashion, especially in contexts with no precedent of large-scale reforms, allowing for flexibility, learning and experimentation, as happened in China (Wei, 1995), chances of achieving better results and local support are higher than where it is executed as a big bang, radical change, as recorded in New Zealand (Gauld, 2000; 2003).

5. Prospects for Privatization

Privatization has and will continue to remain an appealing or compulsory option to many governments for two major sets of reason, to: address extraordinary domestic challenges; and take advantage of external opportunities.

The litany of challenges facing governments world-wide—including, but not limited to: rapid population growth outstripping service delivery; ageing infrastructure; soaring sovereign debt; recession; mounting public-sector wage bill; growing power of public-sector labour unions; widespread discontent with official corruption (real or perceived), 'red tape', partly exposed by the advent of social media; demand for personal freedom; government mistrust; and the general difficulty in finding alternative ways of funding and managing core government activities such as health care, defense, infrastructure (Flynn and Asquer, 2013)—have made privatization a pragmatic solution to these exceptional challenges confronting today's governments, regardless of their ideological leanings.

On the external side, the insistence on economic reforms, including the sale of 'unprofitable' state asserts, deep austerity and deregulation, by donors and lenders, especially the IMF and the World Bank, to crisis-gripped, help-seeking countries; the desire among non-market states to glean the benefits of globalization, including free-trade and investments; political pressure from international human rights and anti-graft organizations, including the UN; and 'contagion effect' from other countries all have a positive influence in luring governments to privatize (more).

Off course, it will be naïve to assume that all states, even if equally facing the above challenges or opportunities, see privatization as the answer. Indeed, in places like South America, the trend seems to be towards re-nationalization, which refers to government takeover of previously sold national assets, usually by force, for multiplicity of reasons, including political, social and economic. The phenomenon, while occurring in almost all nations, both market and non-market based economies, has become more pervasive in Latin America in recent times—all the way from Venezuela to Argentina—where popular dissatisfaction with the distributional impact of privatization, have led to the rise of nationalist governments whose social revolution has become synonymous with large-scale government takeover of important assets and industries, including crude oil and gas, mines, etc and the provision of subsidized goods and services to the poor.

But with corruption becoming rampant, inflation skyrocketing, productivity and output levels dropping, shortage of food and other essential goods becoming frequent, amid soaring crime and increasing local dissatisfaction with government inability to tackle these problems, it is uncertain whether the so-called social revolution can be sustained. The outcome of Venezuela's recent presidential elections, following Chavez's demise, is a case in point. The opposition party, which campaigned on a policy of market-friendly economic reforms, combining elements of privatization and income redistribution, or what is known as the centre left model, came close to winning the elections, proving how public faith in the socialist ideology that once captivated the nation is losing steam in favour of economic liberalization, which include privatization, even if limited. In sum, growing public discontent with the flaws of the socialist system persisting in many non-market states is increasing the prospects of privatization there.

Similarly, even in pro-market economies such as the USA and the UK, recent government bailout of so-called strategic industries, takeover of others and acquisition of majority shares in some entities, amid expanded regulations, in a bid to forestall the recent financial crisis blamed on unfettered markets have raised doubts about the future of (full) privatization. Specific examples include the US government's 2008 takeover of Freddie Mac and Fannir Mae, America's two largest mortgage lenders, in response to the recent credit crunch and the British government's acquisition of the East Coast Line railway franchise from its corporate owners, National Express, in 2009. But again this particular wave of "(re)nationalization" seems to be more pragmatic and temporary, or even a different kind of intervention, than a return to the pre-reform welfare state. For instance, the US government's 'takeover' of the Freddie Mac and Fannir Mae is technically known as conservatorship, and not privatization, because ownership still remains private, except for management which has been put under third party control. Similarly, the UK government has indicated that its acquisition of the East Coast Line railway franchise is only a temporary measure, signaling future return to private ownership.

6. Conclusion

I have examined in this paper the pros and cons of privatization, the decision to handover whole or part of a public enterprise or service to private ownership, including the core efficiency arguments used to justify private ownership of assets and services, and the merits and demerits of such a populist policy. Problems at home, typically drying national coffers, and opportunities outside, especially globalization, plus social change, have made privatization popular with governments. While privatization can help ameliorate some of the pressing problems states face, such as providing revenue for a cash-strapped government, it is by no means a panacea for all the ills of the public sector or the wider society. However, privatization's success will, to large extent, depend on the quality of the political and economic environment within which it occurs and the approach adopted in implementing it. Although there is no one-size-fit-for-all approach to privatization, the key thing is to learn from the good and bad experiences of others, and to apply them to the exigencies of the local context in order to maximize the gains, while minimizing the costs, of privatization. That said, it should be borne in mind that there will always be winners and losers in any privatization policy. The key issue seems not to be whether or not to privatize but where, how, and how much to privatize, so as to distribute its benefits (and costs) equitably. This is where joint ventures and Public-private-partnerships (PPPs) seem to offer some hope to governments. PPPs have emerged as an innovative approach to governments for harnessing the expertise or strengths of the public and private sectors in financing projects, delivering infrastructure and providing services. The major advantage of this policy approach is that it allows both parties, especially governments, to capitalize on the unique advantages of each sector, while sharing or distributing risks equitably. Examples of PPPs include: finance only; build-finance; design-build-finance-maintain; design-build-finance-maintain-operate; build-own-operate; and concession. All approaches are self-explanatory, except perhaps concession, in which the private sector is expected to cede ownership of an investment to government after a certain number of years. PPPs can be regarded as incomplete privatization in many respects, except that the examples listed above are applicable to new projects/programs rather than existing ones. Under joint ventures and PPPs, the government is able to exploit the efficiency of the privates sector or markets while at the same time being able to curb its excesses to certain degree.

References

Appiah-Kubi, K. 2001. 'State-owned Enterprises and Privatization in Ghana' *Journal of Modern African Studies, 39, 197-229*

Bale, M. and T Dale. 1998. 'Public Sector Reform in New Zealand and its relevance to Developing Countries'. *The World Bank Research Observer, 13, 1, 103-121*

Chang, H. 2002. 'Breaking the Mould: An Institutionalist Political Economy Alternative to the Neo-Liberal Theory of the Market and the State. *Cambridge Journal of Economics*, 26, 539-559

DiMaggio, P.J and WW Powell. 1983. 'The Iron Cage Revisited' *American Sociological Review, 48, 147-160*

Flynn, N. 2002. 'Explaining the New Public Management: the Importance of Context. In: K McLoughlin, S Osborne and E Ferlie, 2002 (eds). *New Public Management: Current Trends and Future Prospects.* London: Routledge

Flynn, N. 2011. 'Public Policy and Management: Perspectives and Issues'. *Course Introduction and Overview.* 2ed. London: Centre for Financial and Management Studies, SOAS, University of London

Flynn, N. and A. Asquer. 2013. 'Privatization and Public Private Partnerships'. *Course Introduction and Overview* (eds). London: Centre for Financial and Management Studies, SOAS, University of London

Guriev, S. and W. Megginson. 2005. 'Privatization: What we have learned'. [Online] World Bank. Available from http://siteresources.worldbank.org/DEC/Resources/84797-1251813753820/6415739-1257192350745/gurievmeggison.PDF

Purdon, S. C Lessof and K Woodfield. 2001. 'Research Methods for Policy Evaluation', Department of Works and Pensions Research Working Paper No 2. Crown Copyright, 1-37

Ouchi, W.G. 1980. 'Markets, Bureaucracies and Clans'. *Administrative Science Quarterly, 25*

Schick, A. 1998. 'Why Most Developed Countries Should Not Try New Zeeland Reforms'. *World Bank Observer, 13, 123-131*

Starr, P. 1989. 'The Meaning of Privatization'.

[Online] *Yale Law and Policy Review, 6, 6-41.* Available from

http://www.princeton.edu/~starr/articles/articles80-89/Starr-MeaningPrivatization-88.htm

Udehn, L. 1996. 'Two Approaches to Politics'. In: L. Udehn, 1996

The Limits of Public Choice. London: Routeledge, 17-59

Wei, S-J. 1995. 'From Marx to Markets: China's Economic Reforms as a Megapolicy'. In: J M

Montgomery and D Rondinelli (eds), 1995. *Great Policies: Strategic Innovations in Asia and the*

Pacific Basin. Westport: Praeger, 151-159